ARCHITECTURAL IMPROVISATION:

A History of Vermont's Design/Build Movement 1964–1977

ARCHITECTURAL IMPROVISATION:

A History of Vermont's Design/Build Movement 1964–1977

Edited by Janie Cohen

Essays by Danny Sagan and Kevin Dann

Published by University of Vermont Press
and Robert Hull Fleming Museum,
University of Vermont, Burlington

Distributed by University Press of New England
Hanover and London

Published by University of Vermont Press and Robert Hull Fleming Museum,
University of Vermont, Burlington, on the occasion of the exhibition

ARCHITECTURAL IMPROVISATION:
A History of Vermont's Design/Build Movement 1964-1977
Robert Hull Fleming Museum
September 25–December 19, 2008

Distributed by University Press of New England,
One Court Street, Lebanon, NH 03766. www.upne.com

ISBN 978-0-934658-04-1

COVER: Sibley/Pyramid House, detail
INSIDE COVER: Sketch on Tack House beam (enlarged)
INSIDE BACK COVER: David Sellers, History of Prickly 4th of July Parade Floats
BACK COVER: Tack House, detail

Catalogue Design: Steve Wetherby, Scuola Group

Forty-five years ago, a group of renegade, entrepreneurial young architects and architecture students began to gather in the foothills of Vermont's Green Mountains, seeking creative, professional, and economic freedom in inexpensive land and distance from the country's urban areas. Informed in part by the philosophies and processes of 20th-century artistic movements, Vermont's young design-builders broke free of tradition and constraints at every level. The process they created was as much their legacy as the resulting structures. Those structures, however, soaring up out of hidden hollows in the Mad River Valley of central Vermont, have grown deep roots in Vermont's visual landscape.

A cornerstone of the mission of the University of Vermont's Robert Hull Fleming Museum is to bring to broader audiences the best of Vermont's artistic heritage. This exhibition and catalogue serve that mission, as well as supporting the University of Vermont's commitment to environmental pedagogy. Aesthetically and structurally innovative, the work of the early Design/Build group also represents pioneering efforts in environmentally and socially responsible building, including early experiments with wind energy, solar power, and co-housing.

I want to thank Danny Sagan for serving as Consulting Curator for this exhibition, and former Vermont Folklife Center curator Meg Ostrum for delivering Danny to our doorstep knowing that we shared a deep interest in this subject. Based on extensive interviews and years of study, Danny's curating of the exhibition and his essay in this catalogue help us to understand the history and legacy of this radical architectural movement. Accompanying Danny's essay is a previously unpublished segment from his spirited and wide-ranging 1998 interviews with David Sellers, which encapsulates the architect's creative process. Historian Kevin Dann has contributed an essay to the catalogue that offers an historical, cultural context for our subject, exploring Vermont's draw to creative individuals and groups throughout the 20th century as well as its better-known attraction to those seeking freedoms of all kinds in the late 1960s.

This project is the result of many hands, minds, and generous deeds. We would like to thank the following, who have helped make this project possible: the Kalkin Family Exhibitions Endowment Fund, the 1675 Foundation, the Graham Foundation for Advanced Studies in the Fine Arts, NRG Systems, the University of Vermont's College of Engineering and Mathematical Sciences, TruexCullins, the Walter Cerf Exhibitions Fund, Richard Weintraub and Meredith Ullman Weintraub, and the University of Vermont's Rubenstein School of Environment and Natural Resources. In-kind support has been provided by Small Dog Electronics.

We are grateful for the generosity of many lenders of materials and facilitators of access, including *Architect* and Hanley Wood LLC, Harriet Adams and John Straub, Candy Barr, Dustin Byerly of Goddard College, John Connell, Peter Gluck, Agna Brayshaw, John Hausner, Carol Hosford, Michael Levengood, William Maclay, Jim Sanford, David Sellers, Barry Simpson, and Lester Walker.

We would also like to thank Ellen Wicklum of University Press of New England, and Robert Taylor and Mary-Lou Kete of University of Vermont Press, for their assistance. Finally, my gratitude to the Fleming Museum's extraordinary staff for bringing this complex project to fruition, in particular: Margaret Tamulonis, Interim Curator and Manager of Collections and Exhibitions; Aimee Marcereau DeGalan, the Museum's new Curator of Collections and Exhibitions; and Perry Price, Exhibitions Designer and Preparator. Additionally, I want to thank Chris Dissinger, the Fleming's Public Relations and Marketing Manager, for his assistance with the voluminous visual material for this exhibition and catalogue.

Janie Cohen
Director, Robert Hull Fleming Museum
University of Vermont, Burlington

Much of the research I have conducted on this topic has been in the form of personal interviews. I appreciate the generosity and enthusiasm of the following people, who took the time to talk with me about this history and helped me find the untold stories that enriched and enlarged the scope of the work: Jim Adamson, Steve Badanes, John Connell, Robert Engman, Peter Gluck, John Hausner, Charles Hosford, Daniel Johnson, Louis Mackal, Bill Maclay, John Mallery, Ed Owre, John Rahill, Bill Reineke, John Ringel, Jim Sanford, David Sellers, Barry Simpson, Vance Smith, and Ellen Strauss.

This research has been funded in part by a grant from the Graham Foundation for Advanced Studies in the Fine Arts. I thank the Foundation and also the people who supported my project early on with advice, encouragement, and support: Paul Brouard, John Connell, Meg Ostrum, Jim Schley, and Dan Weese.

Students and recent graduates of Norwich University have devoted hours of work documenting the buildings in Warren and at Goddard. I am indebted to Christine Carroll, Emily Farnsworth, Thornton Hayslett, William Lewis, Heidi McElroy, and Naomi Racinet. Their work was funded by Student Research Fellowships granted by Norwich University

This catalogue and the exhibition would not have been possible without the work of the staff of the University of Vermont's Fleming Museum. I am the beneficiary of the collaborative spirit and tireless efforts of Margaret Tamulonis and Aimee Marcereau DeGalan. Janie Cohen, Director of the Fleming Museum, has been a champion of this topic and an advocate for my research for as long as I have known her. Working together on this project has been a pleasure and a great privilege.

The essay in this catalogue, along with most of the professional efforts of my life, would not be the same with out the steadfast encouragement, enthusiasm, and serious critique of my most appreciated partner in all things design-build as well as in life; thank you Alisa!

Danny Sagan
Consulting Curator

Architectural Improvisation

Danny Sagan

In 1964, three friends from the Yale School of Architecture were skiing at Sugarbush, in Warren, Vermont, when they conceived a plan to become developers, designers, and builders of ski cabins. Two of the friends, David Sellers and Peter Gluck, had previously helped one another on building projects, one for Sellers' brother, and one for Gluck's parents. In Vermont, land was inexpensive and skiing was growing in popularity, so they felt they could take a chance and build speculative projects that they hoped to sell for a profit. David Sellers and his friend William Reineke purchased a piece of land near Warren, now known by the name Prickly Mountain, while Peter Gluck embarked on projects that were designed and built for a site in Bolton, Vermont. From these beginnings a new way of making architecture developed, resulting in structures unmoored from architectural tradition. The design-build architectural movement in Vermont was begun.

The three young architects were motivated by the idea that they could control the economics and construction of their buildings, as well as the design. At the time, Sellers was quoted as saying: "The architect is irresponsible today in . . . that he thinks . . .he has to sit in his office and wait for some client to come up and say, all right build me that. But I think the architect has got to change his whole scope if he's going to survive as an integral part of our future society. I think he's got to play the role of the entrepreneur as well."[1] While the initial development ideas did not produce as much financial success as hoped, Sellers and Reineke created an experiment that did change the "whole scope" of how architecture can be practiced and how buildings can be made. They succeeded in making a place, a community, and a new kind of design culture that lives on to this day.

The exhibition *Architectural Improvisation: A History of Vermont's Design/Build Movement 1964–1977,* and this catalogue that documents it, recognize the design-build experiments at Prickly Mountain as a moment worthy of study both in terms of architectural history and within the context of the cultural history of Vermont. This is not a complete and exhaustive survey; the focus is on a number of examples built in the time period bracketed by the beginning of the first houses in 1964 and the closing of the Design and Construction Program at Goddard College in Plainfield, Vermont, in 1977. We explore and interpret certain architectural events that when seen as part of a greater whole can lead us to an understanding of what has become a lasting legacy. This legacy can be recognized in our built landscape, in the professional lives of people practicing architecture today, in the movement toward more ecologically responsible buildings known as Green Building, and in the way architecture is taught in our schools. The exhibition presents architectural projects that are artifacts of what was then a new and experimental way of making buildings. Some of the buildings are still in use and good condition, others have burned and are documented in archival photographs and drawings. All of these buildings can help us to understand the story of the design-build movement. This catalogue includes research gleaned from articles written at the time of construction, interviews conducted in recent years, and close formal analysis of selected examples of the architecture. It is our hope that a more complete picture will emerge, resulting in a new appreciation of an exceptional architectural movement—one whose structures can still look radical to our eyes today.

Three primary forces launched the design-build experiments at Prickly Mountain: 1) an entrepreneurial urge to create and control one's life economically; 2) a desire to build, to engage in the materiality and empirical nature of architecture with one's own body; and 3) a desire for the creative freedoms and personal expression of the artist's life.

What typically separates the entrepreneur from the professional is a willingness to take on financial risk. The houses built on Prickly Mountain and Gluck's projects were begun as business ventures. Whereas the primary goal was to make money while maintaining design control of the buildings, there was also a thrill in taking on responsibility for the entire project. As Peter Gluck has remarked: "[At that time] we were so optimistic we felt we could do anything."[2] It took nerve to venture beyond the accepted models of architectural practice but the ultimate rewards were independence and artistic freedom.

This freedom allowed the young architects to pursue their architecture in a new way. For Sellers and Reineke this meant being involved in all aspects of the construction. This way of making buildings allowed for a direct connection with the materials used during construction and brought all the senses into the design process. To use the expression "hands-on" is to limit the range of experience. The muscles of the arms, legs, and back were involved in the process; the weight of the materials was always present; the skin, ears, and eyes experienced the sun, wind, and weather as a constant reminder of the forces that nature presents to our buildings. By continually working on the site, the design-builder became a part of the architecture in a way not available to the traditional architect. Sellers and

Reineke were intoxicated with the notion that as designers they could learn from this direct experience. As Reineke explained at the time,

> When you have a joist that you put in that happens to be 6' too long, and [then] you put them all in . . . they may start to develop [into] something. But if you had something drawn, and you cut them up to follow the drawing before you put them all in, that would be it, and you wouldn't learn what the pieces are doing themselves.[3]

These two young architects were predisposed to let the design of their buildings be informed by the construction process, allowing both improvisation and chance to play a role. Ed Owre, a sculptor and Yale graduate who joined them as collaborator on the earliest projects, including the Tack House and the Bridge House, described the theory that guided the process as "Bauhausian:"

> Design is not separate from craft and art . . . and making discoveries by the use, understanding, and [feel of] materials and tools is one way to lead to ideas; rather than the kinds of ideas that are down on paper.[4]

Owre's reference to the Bauhaus is not accidental. Sellers, Reineke, and other of the Prickly Mountain design-builders were exposed to a method of design that had its roots in the renowned design school located in Weimar and Dessau, Germany, in the 1920s. Interestingly, this connection was not made through the Yale School of Architecture, which was run by Paul Rudolph, a student of Walter Gropius (founder of the Bauhaus), but through the Yale School of Art. At the time Sellers and Reineke were at Yale, a young, charismatic sculptor named Robert Engman was teaching the 3-D foundation courses in the art department. Engman had been a student of Josef Albers, who originally developed the foundation courses at the Bauhaus. Albers brought this pedagogy to the Yale School of Art and together with Engman refined the course to fit the short semester system that organized the academic year at Yale.[5] Sellers was introduced to Engman by his friend Duncan Syme who was then at Yale working on an MFA in Sculpture:

> Sellers: [Engman] had a theory of design and a way of teaching it which was magnetic. … He would talk about quality and beauty in a way that was just so clear and so graspable. He had these exercises he would

have you do which would really help you understand it. He didn't just ask you to believe what he said, he would have you try it out.[6]

FIGURE 1: Sketch on Tack House beam

The traditional working model for architects then, as it is now, was to undertake the majority of the design process within the architect's office. All decisions, large and small, were made in the abstract and represented in scale drawings and models. The artist, by contrast, has a method of developing artwork through direct contact with materials. Many sculptors working in the early 1960s, Bob Engman included, would begin a work before the final approach had been completely conceptualized; the experience of working directly with the materials shaped the outcome.

The Tack House, The Sibley/Pyramid House, and the Bridge House were a direct result of a design-build process that resembled the making of art more than the standard methods of making buildings. In architecture firms, projects are completely designed with all details in place before construction begins; final buildings are executed by a builder reading a set of instructions and therefore having no input on the design. By contrast, the houses built on Prickly Mountain were built by their designers, and they were undertaken without the preparation of finished architectural drawings. A broad, formal or structural concept executed as a simple sketch or scale model would often be the only aspect of design completed prior to construction. The process that followed was one of continual design and problem solving (FIGURE 1). It was improvisational and full of surprises; often solutions had to be figured out when the creative process got ahead of practicality. For example, when Ed Owre was building the kitchen in the Tack House, there was insufficient room for the stove or refrigerator. When presented with this problem, Sellers' response was to cut a hole in the wall, cantilever the floor, and cover the "bump out" with curved Plexiglas, thereby extending the kitchen[7] (FIGURE 2).

FIGURE 2

While each of the houses discussed is a built expression of the design-build ethos that was developing on Prickly Mountain, the Tack House served as a living model for the lifestyle that would endure. The house became a locus of work, relaxation, eating, and sleeping, for the design-builders as well as for others. As an integrated living/working space that became Sellers' home for many years, it stands as one of the first examples of a design-build office.

To practice design-build, one needed to be willing to live with design accidents. The design-builder was expected to make mistakes, experience their impact, and learn from them. The Tack House remains as one of the best examples

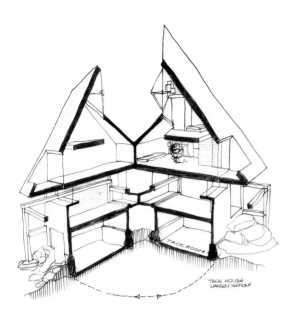

FIGURE 3: David Sellers, drawing of Tack House, 1969

of this improvisational architectural process. Parts of the building are salvaged from an old sugar house, including the lower frame, which is exposed on the outside and then disappears into the interior (FIGURE 3). Some of the siding appears as if it were salvaged from an old barn, yet the profile of the building bears no recognizable relationship to any local agricultural buildings. The house does not read as a conceptual whole from any angle. As you move around it, as with a piece of sculpture, its formal composition and its profile against the sky change. From certain views it almost seems unclear whether it is a finished building; it appears more like a strange piece of machinery parked temporarily in a field (PLATE 1). We cannot analyze the building as a fixed object in time and space, as it evolved from an active process rather than from a predetermined idea or concept. In 1965, the building method taking shape on Prickly Mountain was the architectural equivalent of the contemporaneous artistic movement known as Process Art. It was the *act* of design-build that interested these architects, more than the finished product.

The process of building the house as a collaborative effort was also of great interest to those involved. Ed Owre remembers:

> . . . the Tack House gave us a way to work together. We learned more from each other when we were working together than we [would have] sitting around making drawings, and I don't remember anybody sitting around making drawings. It just wasn't part of it.[8]

This sense of collaboration and community, the act of learning from one another, living near one another, and working together was different from the ways architects were practicing at the time. One of the strongest outgrowths and lasting legacies of the original work on Prickly Mountain is the idea that buildings can result from a process that is collaborative and communal.

To view the Tack House after 40 years of weather, fires, and additions one can still recognize the original structure as an independent component that stands next to its mutational kindred additions (PLATES 2, 3). Sellers speaks of every design having a "seed" or "DNA" from which the rest of the building gets its formal language. The design-builder begins with a strong and flexible concept model that allows him to improvise while maintaining a coherent design. The original Tack House is the generative "seed" for the additions that followed and it retains a recognizable identity as a separate part of the compositional whole. In this aspect it has its roots in an older way of building, that of the 19th-century connected farmhouses of northern New England (FIGURE 4). These older structures developed as a series of connected volumes, growing into the landscape from the original farmhouse. The primary purpose for connecting the farmhouse to the barns was the harsh climate, and this way of building has become identified with a particular region. Similarly, the Tack House, by growing in this way, became rooted to its site and deeply connected to this northern New England setting.

FIGURE 4

The Sibley/Pyramid House, which from some angles appears to be growing out of Prickly Mountain like an extension of the underlying bedrock, is a particularly successful example of the early design-build experiments. It owes its more discrete appearance to the fact that it was designed as a formal whole early in the process and has had no subsequent additions. John Mallery, Reineke's collaborator in construction and future business partner, once remarked that the design concept was to create a building whose floor-plans and exterior elevation drawings would look very similar to one another (FIGURE 5).[9] The true sophistication of the design lies in the simplicity of the composition of the volumes that was achieved through the formal methods of addition and subtraction. The form is that of a cube, in this case 16' on each edge, with triangular additions radiating out from the cube both into the landscape and up to the sky (PLATES 5, 6). The exterior is covered on the roofs as well as the walls with clapboards that were applied with a greater than typical overlap, giving the building a tight, consistent skin (COVER IMAGE).

FIGURE 5: Bill Reineke, drawing of Sibley/Pyramid House, 1967

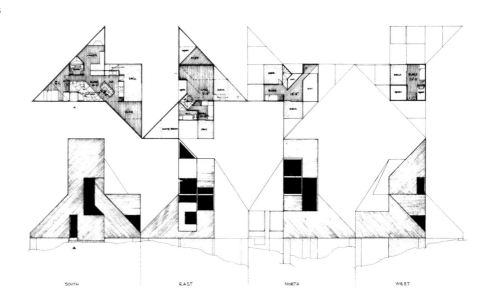

SOUTH   EAST   NORTH   WEST

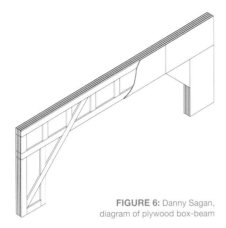

FIGURE 6: Danny Sagan, diagram of plywood box-beam

DIED: Jan. 18, 1978, The Bridge House, at Prickley Mt., age 12.

Last week the Bridge House burned to the ground. For a handful of afficionados it means the passing of a manifestation of dreams and a massive experiment in exploring space, light, sculpture, color, texture, materials, and man's relation to what he makes.

A wall of bedrooms, a bed cantalevered into the trees, southlight scoops, stressed-skin plywood structures.

Two, 100 foot bridges intersecting in the middle of the house . . .

End grain plywood floors, castings from salvaged farm machinery used as steps, chairs, doorknobs, bowl mill sinks and seats . . .

The 24 foot long single pieces of plastic for a panoramic view

The thirty foot cantalevers and 60 foot spans on the bridges . . . all these were part of the house.

"This house is to the traditional, chalet style lodge as a Raushenberg is to a Turner landscape," (Life Magazine, 1968).

But the most wonderful thing about the house was the manner in which it was built, for it began as a test of the relation of an architect and a sculptor and how they could integrate their skills and talents, the composition of forms, color, texture, and materials, with light, structure, space and function.

First, was to forget about designing the house and go right to building it, so the sculpture is integrated into the action of the form from the beginning.

Starting with sculptor Ed Owre, now on the faculty of the University of Vermont, and architect David Seller, more than a dozen painters, sculptors, and architects from across the United States participated in the creation.

The Bridge House was among the first in a style of action-buildings and reality-oriented artistic statements which are still emerging in the U.S. today.

Speaking for many, we are sorry to see her gone, but the value behind the experience of the house can never be lost, and we are all the better for it.

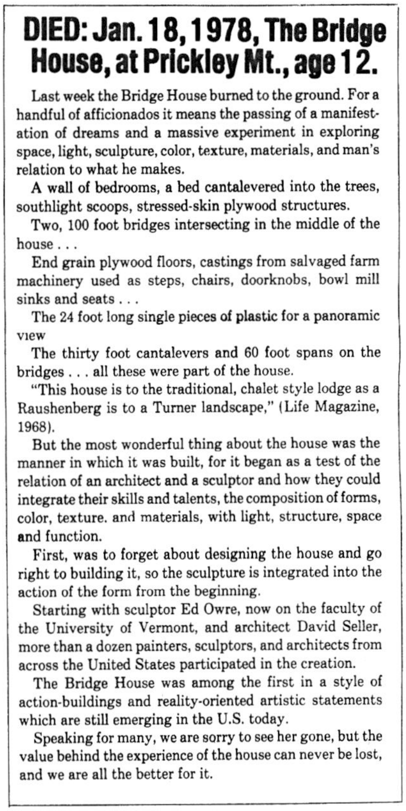

FIGURE 7: *Valley Reporter,* January, 1978

Upon entering the interior, it becomes apparent that the building is organized as a composition of planes. Interior walls are pierced and corner windows reveal the nature of the exterior structure (PLATES 7, 8). These wall planes are the key to the design in that they also resist most of the forces exerted on the building, including the vertical loads. The walls and the interior supporting members were constructed using a method known as plywood/laminate beams or, more generically, plywood box-beams. Structural loads that in the past would have been carried by very large, solid wooden beams or heavy, expensive steel structures, are carried instead by relatively lightweight beams. These beams are composed of small, wooden members that act as flanges and plywood skins that serve as webs, which tie the structure together (FIGURE 6). This allowed the builders to construct a very strong, lightweight structure out of easily acquired materials that could be lifted into place with little effort. If, as the design changed, the beams needed to be modified to carry heavier loads, this could be accomplished by adding more plywood skins. The internal structure of the box-beam, made of 2 x 10' and 2 x 12' lumber, could also be extended beyond the profile of the beam to allow for future improvisation. This idea of extending pieces of the construction into space for future, yet to be determined use, came to be known by the nickname "Wild Beam Theory." The box-beam technology, with its flexibility and strength, became the primary method of carrying loads in many of the design-build projects that followed.

Looking at the original schematic drawings of the Sibley/Pyramid House, we can see that the profile and certain aspects of the building changed during construction. While the improvisational process ties this house to the Tack House and Bridge House both formally and historically, the Sibley/Pyramid House was the most articulated and complete design to emerge from the early houses at Prickly Mountain. At its most basic, it is a crystalline formation perfect in its geometry, humanized by the random effects of weather, construction, and site. It is architecture generated by an artistic process that was allowed to continue through construction.

The Bridge House, which burned in 1978 (FIGURE 7), embodied the improvisational spirit of design-build as well as the lifestyle of its occupants. A weekend retreat for skiers, the interior spaces contained the twists, turns, and inclined planes one expects to find on a ski slope.

The house was organized around a large gathering space that connected to distant views of the mountains through very large windows. The inhabitants of the house moved through the space vertically, using steep stairs and climbing rungs that allowed them to occupy the walls (FIGURE 8). Once high up, they settled themselves into hidden sitting-shelves and sleeping-cubbies. The huge glass wall was made of separate pieces, some of which were placed at oblique angles; some of the walls and ceilings were sloped at steep angles. All of these components worked together to reinforce a dynamic sense of movement within the space.

FIGURE 8: Bridge House interior, 1967

The structure, literally perched on the slope (PLATE 9), was attached to the hillside with two long, wooden bridges. These bridges, which continued into the interior space of the house, were made with plywood box-beams, and their length demonstrated a willingness to push the structural limitations of this technology (PLATES 10, 12). Looking at a photograph taken during construction, we can also see the "wild beams" extending beyond the shell of the structure into the space of the landscape (FIGURE 9). The design-builders of the Bridge House had experimental opportunities that were unusual and exhilarating for architects at the time. Their work with the materials of construction led them to a structural technology that perfectly suited their process and allowed them the flexibility and creative freedom that they craved.

The two projects by Peter Gluck presented in the exhibition are useful to look at in the context of the works originating at Prickly Mountain. After collaborating with Sellers early on, Gluck chose not to move to Warren. A self-described "Urbanist," Gluck moved to New York City and based his practice there. The house he built in Vermont, which was called ARDEC (Architectural Research and Development), was conceived as an experimental prototype to be built out of a series of pre-fabricated panels and large box-shaped building sections (PLATES 13, 14). It was designed in New York and the panels and boxes were then built during the winter in a Vermont lumberyard by local carpenters who were otherwise out of work due to seasonal slow-downs. This was a departure from the process that was developing at Prickly Mountain. Gluck designed the project in such a way that the parts would be simple enough to build that "any guy could

FIGURE 9: Bridge House construction, 1966

FIGURE 10: ARDEC House construction

make these panels."[10] The panels and boxes were then transported to the site and lifted into place by crane (FIGURE 10).

FIGURE 11: ARDEC House model

The ARDEC House and the larger-scale apartment building for which it was a model both have a clear logic based in diagrammatic thinking. Both the simple model of the project (FIGURE 11) and the house's relationship to the site show that the house was far more predetermined before construction than any house built on Prickly Mountain. While there was room within his system for variation and invention, Gluck was less interested in the kind of improvisational process going on in Warren. Nor was he interested in making houses that were singular works of art. He was, and still is, committed to creating architectural solutions for multi-unit housing and to delivering high quality by controlling the construction process.[11]

The ARDEC House proved that a small house could be a laboratory for building systems used in larger projects. It was a well-designed house built efficiently on a difficult site, and the house sold easily. An entrepreneurial success, it served as one model for practicing design-build. Unlike the other projects in the exhibition however, the ARDEC House was not a vehicle for artistic expression. The final product is subdued and refined; its form grows from the method that built it and the house feels somewhat removed from the landscape and the site upon which it is built. The experience of being on site in Vermont did not inspire Gluck to become connected to the landscape of Vermont, and ultimately he did not become part of the design-build community of Warren.

With coverage in magazines and newspapers and growing public awareness of their work, Sellers and Reineke were able to inspire more young architects like themselves come to Warren. They offered to sell parcels of land to young designers provided that the new construction was "experimental." In a *New York Times* article published in January of 1966, Sellers' said, " We're encouraging other young architects and architectural students who are doing interesting work to buy land here and build either for their own use or to sell."[12]

They developed a master plan, dividing up the mountain into lots. Some of the lots were designated for cluster housing and much of the open land was reserved for common use including a pond, pasture, and ski and hiking trails (FIGURE 12).

Architecture students and young architects responded to Sellers' and Reineke's open, adventurous, and entrepreneurial approach to design by migrating to Vermont. The earliest arrivals were from Yale School of Architecture, including Charles Hosford and Barry Simpson. John Hausner came to Prickly Mountain from Washington University in St. Louis, where the Bauhaus method was at the core of the architectural curriculum.[13]

The culture of invention and collaboration grew and informal partnerships developed. These new collaborative teams designed and built houses, started businesses, and created design-build operations that could travel to remote sites. The location for many of these new businesses was an old factory in downtown Warren known as the Bobbin Mill (FIGURE 13).

The Bobbin Mill, purchased in 1970 by Sellers, Barry Simpson, and their friend Fred Steele, became the hub of many activities associated with the Prickly Mountain community. Occupants included architecture offices for Sellers, Simpson, Hosford, and others. There was woodworking shop-space for Union Woodworks and other cabinetmakers such as Randy Taplin, as well as office and fabrication space for two woodstove companies including Vermont Castings. Northwind Power (a manufacturer of wind turbines) began at the Bobbin Mill. Two young architects, Mack Rood and Rob Bast, made experimental waterless toilets of fiberglass. In the early 1970s, at any one time there could be more than 30 people working in the Bobbin Mill, making stoves, furniture, windmills, and parts of houses, as well as designing architecture. The culture of design-build transformed a structure from the old economy of Vermont—textiles—into an incubator for what would become the next economy: energy-efficient stoves, renewable energy generators, fine crafted furniture, composting toilets, and innovative architectural design.

One of the projects that emerged from this incubator was the Lovejoy House on Lake Honnedaga in New York State, designed by Barry Simpson and built in pieces at the Bobbin Mill. The construction involved assembling a series of prefabricated panels on site to support a horizontal plywood box-beam that in turn supported a cable roof suspended in between. This roof structure took the shape of a catenary curve similar in concept to Paul Rudolph's Cocoon House in Sarasota, Florida, and Eero Saarinen's design for Dulles Airport. This roof profile, efficient in

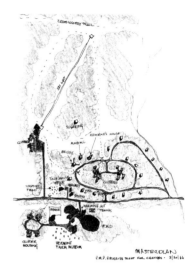

FIGURE 12: David Sellers, drawing of plan for Prickly Mountain, 1966

FIGURE 13: Bobbin Mill, Warren, Vermont, ca. 1970

FIGURE 14: Living on the Lovejoy House site, sleeping structure by Steve Badanes

FIGURE 15: Silver Bullet

FIGURE 16: Dimetrodon wind turbine

its use of structure because the thin steel cables work in tension, is also the perfect shape for a roof on a house in the snow belt of the Adirondacks; the inverted curve channels the wind which blows off the snow (PLATE 15).

This small, prefabricated house with an experimental roof is exemplary of the innovative designs coming out of Warren at the time (PLATE 16). The house was completed with Simpson living on the site during construction. He formed an expeditionary building team that devoted two summers to the construction of the building. This was the design-build experience at its most Romantic, in the sense that it involved the artist's retreat to the wilderness and the creation of his own primal dwelling on the wooded site (FIGURE 14).

During the construction of this house, Simpson was joined by Michael Goldfinger, Bob Magilvray, and Steve Badanes. Badanes, a college friend of Simpson, later went on to found the long-surviving, nomadic design-build outfit, Jersey Devil, a company known for its members' practice of living and working in remote building sites. Badanes credits his experiences with Simpson as giving him the idea to create Jersey Devil along this model.[14]

Living on the site during construction has been a common experience in the history of design-build. Beginning at Prickly Mountain, builders of projects have lived on or near the building site; Simpson pushed the limits by experimenting with minimal living accommodations. His first dwelling, which for ten years he shared with his wife and children, was a very small, movable structure known as the "Silver Bullet." In its largest iteration, the Silver Bullet was only 230 square feet of enclosed space (FIGURE 15). As Simpson and his family began to raise most of their own food on their land, the practice of living on the site transformed to living within the site. While ecological design was not one of the original stated goals of Sellers and Reineke when they first moved to Warren, it became one of the larger themes and values guiding the design-build community as it developed over time.

The Dimetrodon project exemplifies the commitment to a more environmentally responsive architecture. Inspired by a lecture and an invitation by Sellers, three students in the architecture program at the University of Pennsylvania moved to Vermont in 1970 and started building the experimental structure they named after a pelycosaur they had seen at the Museum of Natural History, which could heat and cool itself using a large, spiny fin on its back (FIGURE 16).

An early experiment in cohousing, Dimetrodon was a structure of private dwelling units organized around a courtyard with shared public amenities, including gardens (PLATE 17). It was one of the earliest prototypes of this kind of intentional community, which was also being developed in Europe at the time; the earliest examples are cited as being the Sættedammen and Skraplanet projects built in Denmark from 1968 to 1972.[15] In the United States, cohousing did not take off until a decade and a half after the project in Warren was undertaken.

The Dimetrodon project was begun by William Maclay, Jim Sanford, and Richard Travers, who were later joined by Sucosh Norton, Ellen Strauss, and Hito Coleman. Designed as a series of giant parallel box-beam trusses, the project was organized around the concept that residents would receive services such as sewer, water, electricity, and heat, and construct their own dwelling in the space between the box beams. Each occupant determined how many levels were needed for living space. The south side of the building was predetermined to be a large wall of solar collectors (PLATES 18, 19); the exterior skin on the north, east, and west face of each unit was designed by the occupants (PLATES 20, 21). The collective result is a giant collage that is both thrilling and chaotic. The spirit of self-reliance combined with shared community values comes together in a whole that was, and remains, dynamic, visionary, and supportive of a new lifestyle.

Dimetrodon was innovative in its use of renewable energy. In its early years it made use of wind power for electricity. The heat-source was two-fold: a site-built, wood-burning boiler; and an enormous water-trickling, thermal solar collector that was installed on the majority of the south facing slope of the building. In developing the design of this collector, Maclay traveled to seek out the advice of experts in the field such as Dr. Maria Telkes, the pioneering solar inventor.[16] True to the spirit of the times, the builders took it upon themselves to research, design, and implement the systems that were needed. As Jim Sanford put it: "The reason we did it was because no one was teaching it."[17] The building was mechanically conceived with a sophistication and complexity unusual for its time. Dimetrodon added to the culture of Prickly Mountain the motif of architect as scientist-inventor. It is also worthy to note here that this project was conceived and implemented *before* the Oil Shock of 1973.

In the intervening years, the wind turbine has been removed and the trickling collectors have been replaced by passive solar glass that adds light as well as heat to the living spaces. The wood boiler, however, survives, and it has become a symbol of community. Unlike most Americans living in single-family homes or apartment houses with a paid superintendent, the members of the Dimetrodon community share the physical responsibilities of maintaining the building. Each family agrees to stoke the boiler during the winter, reinforcing the residents' commitment to one another and their reliance on the group.

The development of a community with a shared social life but private living spaces stands out as one of the most important outcomes of the Dimetrodon project. Contemporaneous with Vermont's commune movement, the project nurtured the best of communal life while avoiding its pitfalls. Dimetrodon was originally planned to hold thirteen units, but only half of the original master plan was realized; the building to this day accommodates five families with one unit as a shared community house, which is sometimes rented. For the families who have lived in the complex, feeling part of a community is one of the most successful aspects of the design. A concrete example of how innovative design can have a positive impact on people's lives, the move to concentrate six families in one building on thirteen acres not only allowed room for a garden, an orchard, and open space, it also created a place that takes on the best qualities of village life.

Dimetrodon is one of the earliest examples of a multifamily project in Vermont having a primary goal of being environmentally responsible. Its creators wished to and succeeded in providing "… a working model for a more sound pattern for growth."[18] Bill Maclay, among others, continued this work and ultimately went on to design some of the earliest high-performing, energy-efficient, multifamily housing built in Vermont. Dimetrodon helped to set the stage for Vermont's emergence today as a center for the Green Building movement.

Another early design-build cohousing project that focused on solar design and energy efficiency was Anthos, located in Waitsfield, Vermont. Initially the idea of Charles Hosford in 1972, Anthos was a collaboration among Hosford, John Hausner, Tom Amsler, and Charles Haggenaugh. In this project, the architects joined forces and capital, acting as developers and builders for clients, themselves included. Some of the designers already had children, therefore the dwelling units were larger than those at Dimetrodon and more easily accommodated the needs of growing families. The interior architecture incorporated some remarkable spatial experiences that continued the inventiveness, artistic creativity, and daring of the earlier structures built on Prickly Mountain (PLATES 24, 25). Anthos also created architectural solutions that showed a more mature approach to energy efficiency, structural durability, and comfort for occupants wanting to live in Vermont year-round.

Anthos is based on a strategy similar to Dimetrodon, where the individual units are divided by vertical, structural planes composed of enormous plywood box-beams. This model of dividing dwelling units with structural walls is quite old; examples can be found in the compact townhouse developments of 18th- and 19th-century city neighborhoods. Anthos updated this model for the rural landscape by responding sensitively to the land on which it was built. The building is sited on the edge of an open pasture where the grade slopes down steeply to the south. The building profile is a large triangle like Dimetrodon; in this case, the hypotenuse of the triangle faces the pasture to the north and rises gently, as an extension of the ground plane (PLATE 22). This allowed for a large vertical wall to be built on the south, which became the side of the structure most expressive of the individuality of each occupant (PLATE 23). The designers also made good use of passive solar architecture by opening up this south wall with glass and terraces. The building is an update of a house form developed by European settlers as a response to the New England climate. It resembles, in diagrammatic profile, a classic Saltbox house with a long, protective roof to the north and a tall, sun-absorbing wall on the south.

Anthos anticipated a strategy of the cohousing movement—the shared common space—which in this case was placed under the building. While this placement is unusual, a covered space for cars, equipment, and a rainy-day play-area for kids is a sensible and useful architectural response to the northern New England winters. As neighbors come and go they casually meet each other, while the children all share a protected territory where they can be as loud and messy as they wish regardless of weather.

Anthos is a vibrant dwelling place thirty-six years after its inception. There are still residents living in the complex who were part of the original construction: couples that have raised their children there and now live as empty-nesters. The structure has successfully accommodated the individual needs of its occupants while encouraging lasting community. Integrated with the site, it responds intelligently to the heating and cooling needs required by the climate. The initial structural strategy that grew out of the design-build process has been a flexible framework here, allowing for architectural improvisation while presenting a coherent and unified building.

In the fall of 1970, concurrent with the evolution of Dimetrodon, Anthos, and the activities at the Bobbin Mill, there was another hub for alternative and creative thinking developing in the town of Plainfield, Vermont. Goddard College, which at the time was a center for innovative teaching and experimental models for learning, began planning a design school. At the request of Goddard President Gerry Witherspoon, John Mallery (an alumnus of the Yale School of Architecture and Prickly Mountain) and David Sellers helped the College embark on a design education program that was compatible with Goddard's pedagogy of "experiential learning" and was based on the methods developed at Prickly Mountain.

Sellers, Mallery, and the students began by building the Design Center (PLATE 26). This building is centrally organized as a three-story, open-plan workspace with many different interior levels (PLATE 27) culminating in a glass-surrounded meeting space at the top (PLATE 28). The construction method was to erect the primary structure first to the full height of the building and enclose spaces as required. The main columns and beams were made of layers of smaller dimensional lumber ganged together. This system, ideal for a pedagogical project, is a reinterpretation of traditional timber framing transformed to accommodate many enthusiastic yet unskilled builders. It provided the flexibility desired for an experimental project as well as a new testing ground for Sellers' Wild Beam Theory.

The Design Center resulted from a design-build methodology where the building was "conceived as a continuing process which grew from day to day, without need for formal working drawings as ideas became material realities."[19] The students at Goddard were learning to approach architecture primarily as building, which gave them daily physical contact with the materials and methods of construction. This teaching methodology grew directly from the philosophy of Sellers and Mallery, who outlined their reasons as follows:

> [T]he architectural profession suffers a real drawback in that architects, who rarely build the buildings they design, deal less directly with their medium than most other groups involved in the arts. The [traditional] student suffers a double disadvantage in that he is required to spend years working out imaginary solutions to artificial problems that have little if anything to do with reality.[20]

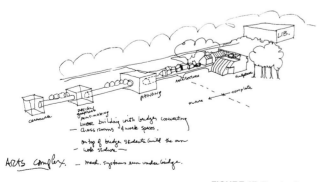

FIGURE 17: Drawing for Goddard College Arts Complex

With the success of the Design Center, the College began the much more ambitious project of designing and building a Linear Arts Complex which would include two very large buildings, the Painting Building and the Sculpture Building, connected by a bridge (FIGURE 17; PLATES 29, 30). These projects offered the opportunity to demonstrate that the design-build process could produce large facilities to accommodate institutional activities. Collaborative groups conceived the buildings with simple models and drawings, and then constructed them by engaging in an ongoing process of design and deliberation. These large buildings were organized around their primary structure; this involved the design and placement of very large plywood box-beams creating impressive spans that provided large, open space for many varied activities.

These projects and their methodology fit the zeitgeist of Goddard. The direct engagement with building met the requirement of *experiential* learning. The day-to-day experimentation and improvisation suited the College's desire to remove traditional restraints from the students. A brochure written at the time describing the program also shows that the curriculum offered opportunities to engage in collaborative problem-solving with real results:

> Faculty, students, and staff of the Goddard College Design and Construction Program are committed to explore, discuss, and investigate possible means for relevant intervention in the man-made environment. Program participants become directly engaged with tools, materials, themselves, and with others in combinations required for assembling a structure. Whenever there is a choice we move to the arena of real buildings, real problems, and real people.[21]

This desire for "relevant intervention in the man-made environment" inspired two young architecture students studying at Harvard's Graduate School of Design to leave their studies in Cambridge and move to Plainfield. Vance Smith and John Rahill, who would later become integral players in the creative economy of Vermont, were becoming alienated from their institution and began to focus their school projects on energy efficiency; they received no support from their professors.[22] The watershed moment, as Smith describes it, came during the construction of the new building for Harvard's design school:

> The Architecture School was housed in the yard of Robinson Hall and across the street Harvard was building Gund Hall, this brand new marvelous edifice, for zillions and zillions of dollars (FIGURE 18). The cost overruns were becoming scandalous, and for some reason, I don't remember how, we heard about these guys at Goddard who were building their own building. The contrast of intention and the irony involved was too much for us.[23]

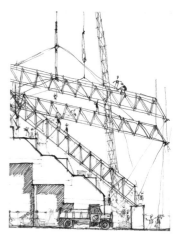

FIGURE 18: Vance Smith, drawing of Gund Hall construction, Harvard University

Smith and Rahill joined the building projects at Goddard as graduate students. While John Mallery was working with undergraduates constructing the Painting Building, the graduate students were left alone to construct the drafting studio on the bridge. They were almost as on their own as Sellers and Reineke had been in the early years of Prickly Mountain. John Rahill, who later was a founding partner in the Montpelier, Vermont, architecture firm Black River Design, remembers that during his days at Goddard there was not much supervision and there were many mistakes made. This environment, however unconventional, was an effective way to learn, according to Rahill. For him, Goddard became a place to experiment and to learn both from mistakes and successes. For Smith, who later became an architect in Vermont and a designer for Vermont Castings Stove Company, the experience was equally freeing. She recounts that it was at Goddard within the community of design-build that she first learned to be ". . . fearless about taking a hammer and building something."[24] The end result for both Rahill and Smith was liberation from the constraints they had felt at Harvard.

The Design and Construction Program at Goddard College ended in 1977. The buildings that came out of this program are remarkable in their size and in the flexibility and unpredictability of the process that produced them. They were built almost entirely by a large and varied group of students, some of who were practicing construction work for the first time. While some may question the long-term viability of the buildings themselves, the opportunities that they provided as a testing ground for a generation preoccupied with freedom from the status quo and a zeal for new methods of collaboration and engagement was rare and seminal.

Today, design-build as pedagogy has become almost a normative requirement in the minds of young architecture students. There is presently a renaissance of design-build programs in architecture schools across the country, some receiving much acclaim and achieving remarkable results. Some of these programs utilize consensus and experimentation as part of the design, making them inheritors of the method as it was originated at Goddard. Looking out across the landscape, it is hard to imagine that in 1964 there were no construction programs within the architecture schools; when the Goddard program was begun, the few programs that have become long-established were also in their infancy. We can see that one of the important legacies of the Prickly Mountain group is this trend toward the inclusion of design-build classes within our schools of architecture. In the state of Vermont, this legacy has been institutionalized at the Yestermorrow Design/Build School, located in Warren.

Yestermorrow was founded by John Connell in 1980 as a place for architects, homeowners, architecture students, and builders to learn many different aspects of the design-build process. Connell, who moved to Warren to work with Sellers, created an institution that sets itself apart from other schools in that it includes in its philosophy the value that "every designer should know how to build and every builder should know how to design."[25] It is also guided by an ethic of inclusion that has its roots deep in the rocky soils of Prickly Mountain. By resisting the model of education that creates dependence, Yestermorrow is a place where anyone can learn how to use tools for design and construction, while developing personal, professional, and creative independence.

FIGURE 19: Yestermorrow, Waitsfield 10

Yestermorrow has always been committed to continuing the design-build tradition of collaborative problem solving. This practice is embodied in one of the early projects of the school: the house known as the Waitsfield 10 is one of the best examples of the Prickly Mountain tradition (FIGURE 19). It began as a conceptual design experiment based on a foundation plan of a rotated square, which became the section diagram for the house. As the house rises from its minimal footprint, it turns to travel horizontally through space and becomes metaphorically un-built as the inside volume transforms into an outdoor deck space, as solid walls turn to frames and lattice, ending in the landscape as one column supporting the end of a plywood box-beam. The house serves as a metaphor for the design-build process where finishing the job is sometimes in conflict with the joys of building. It is appropriate that the house included in its construction the labor of many people who only participated in the middle of the process. As a pedagogical exercise involving many small classes over a 16-year period (1984–2000), it is safe to assume it is the work of over 100 people.

Yestermorrow continues to perpetuate the early values of Prickly Mountain: 1) independence, 2) learning through the construction process, and 3) making buildings as a form of artistic expression. As the ethos of the design-build movement embraced environmental stewardship and collaboration as key values in the making of architecture, the school evolved to become a leader in architectural pedagogy by integrating these principles into its curriculum. Today many of the practitioners who started at Prickly Mountain participate in public programs and teach in the classrooms on the campus of Yestermorrow.

Vermont's design-build movement has a rich legacy. Many of the practitioners are still working as architects in Vermont either for themselves or in larger firms. The Yestermorrow campus (Bill Maclay), NRG Systems' production facility in Hinesburg (Maclay), the Pitcher Inn in Warren (David Sellers), the Montpelier Police Department (Black River Design/Bill Reineke), and the Aiken Center (Maclay) on the campus of the University of Vermont (planned construction start 2009), are all large, public buildings designed by architects who began their careers on Prickly Mountain and at Goddard College. John Hausner, whose first house still stands on Prickly Mountain, created Homestead Design Inc., an employee-owned, vertically integrated design, construction, and real estate company responsible for many units of affordable housing, commercial construction, and planned development in the greater Burlington area. Many of the businesses that started in the Bobbin Mill are still producing stoves (Vermont Castings), handmade toys (Dirt Road), wind turbines (Northwind Power), fine crafted wood products, and business furniture (Wall/Goldfinger). Some of the business people who got their start at the Bobbin Mill are now running new companies in Vermont that purvey products as diverse as computers (Small Dog Electronics) and sleds (Mad River Rocket).

Many of the Prickly Mountain alumni have served as selectboard members in Warren and Waitsfield, and there have been representatives in the Vermont State Legislature who can trace their bloodlines back to the design-build movement. Charles Hosford went on to create and run an international peace organization called Project Harmony, which has the stated goal of creating ". . . a world where individuals and communities collaborate across borders to resolve global challenges . . . where solutions are . . . strengthened by individuals empowered with skills and knowledge."[26]

What started as a small group of renegade, young architects on a remote hillside in Warren became a movement that has enriched the built landscape of Vermont with many examples of innovative architecture, lasting institutions that empower communities and individuals, and new models for socially and environmentally responsible businesses. Like the commune movement, the social ecologists, and the organic farmers, the architects of the design-build movement have helped to make Vermont a place that thrives by continual improvisation, by adapting to changing social, economic, environmental, and cultural realities in creative ways that address need and strengthen community.

Endnotes

1. C. Ray Smith, "Architecture Swings Like a Pendulum Do," *Progressive Architecture,* May 1966, 150

2. Danny Sagan, unpublished interview with Peter Gluck, 2008

3. C. Ray Smith, "Architecture Swings Like a Pendulum Do," *Progressive Architecture,* May, 1966, 153

4. Danny Sagan, unpublished interview with Ed Owre, 2004

5. Danny Sagan, unpublished interview with Robert Engman, 2004

6. Danny Sagan, interview with David Sellers, 1998, previously published in *Influence across Fields, The Chicago Architectural Club Journal,* 2001, Volume 10

7. Danny Sagan, unpublished interview with Ed Owre, 2004

8. Ibid.

9. Danny Sagan, unpublished interview with John Mallery, 2004

10. Danny Sagan, unpublished interview with Peter Gluck, 2008

11. Ibid.

12. "2 Architects Put Plans Into Action; Turn Builders as They Test Ideas in Vermont Hills Way-Out House Is Built Way Up [sic]," *New York Times,* January 30, 1966, R1

13. Danny Sagan, unpublished interview with John Hausner, 2000

14. Danny Sagan, unpublished interview with Steven Badanes, 2006

15. Kathryn McCammant & Charles Durrett, *Cohousing, A Contemporary Approach to Housing Ourselves* (Ten Speed Press, Berkeley CA, 1988)

16. Danny Sagan, unpublished interview with William Maclay, 2008

17. "A Condo Before Its Time." *Home,* 24 April 1991, 144

18. William Maclay Architects & Planners website: www.wmap-aia.com

19. David A. Morton, "Organic Architecture at Goddard College," *Progressive Architecture,* November, 1971, 90

20. Ibid., 90

21. Goddard College pamphlet, 1970s

22. Danny Sagan, unpublished interview with John Rahill, 2006

23. Danny Sagan, unpublished interview with Vance Smith, 2004

24. Ibid.

25. Yestermorrow Design/Build School website: www.yestermorrow.org

26. Project Harmony website: www.projectharmony.org

David Sellers interviewed by Danny Sagan

December 1998

Sellers: Fred Steele was a classmate at mine at Yale—an eccentric, extremely brilliant guy. He was called "Pinhead." He came up with the idea that he and I should collaborate on a house for him. . . . we would build this house; we would invent it while we were building it. He was really into the process and he wrote a piece that related to this, because he was very interested in creativity.[1] He studied with a guy at Yale named Chris Argyris, who wrote a book called *Personality and Organization*.[2] This was the first management guide on the personality and growth and self-reliance and self-worth: what that has to do with productivity and how that makes you do good work. Chris taught these courses at Yale that were totally amazing. Pinhead was his star pupil and went to on to write books of his own [and to teach at Harvard and Yale]. He wrote this book called *Sense of Place* and used this building as a vehicle[3] . . . Yale alumni magazine published this house[4] [as did *Progressive Architecture*[5]]. It was also published in *Glamour* magazine; they had all these models up there lounging around the house (laughs).[6]

So in the process of designing this house, I told Pinhead that we can't figure out what the living room is going to be like until we get the roof on. So we built the whole house all the way to the top; not only was there no living room, there was no living room floor, no living room structure. The walls went down to the ground. There was just dirt and rocks and scaffolding. And I couldn't figure out what it was going to be like. Pinhead thought this was really cool and he came up with this theory that the longer you wait, the higher the probability of creativity.

Sagan: The longer you wait?

Sellers: The longer you can stay unresolved. He held classes on irresolution and helping people to live with [ambiguity], but still being able to proceed and move forward. This house was a good test of that.

So I hired Tom Luckey. And I finally figured out what to do [with the floor]. I said, let's build a lot of chunks, sculptural chunks; this might have come out of Le Corbusier and the Modular. I said, let's build some sculptural pieces that we'll bolt together and put some foam and carpeting on it, and that will be the floor. The sizes and proportions of these things will be based on the size of your arm and what sitting posture is and standing and walking up stairs, because there had to be a stairway too. The idea was that you would go from the kitchen to this environment, and you could dive into it because it was padded; any place that you sat or lay down, it would fit your body (FIGURE 20). We worked on that, we got Tom Luckey to build it, and it came out great. It really worked, it was a spectacular thing. Pinhead held a lot of seminars there, people would come up and lounge around on this floor.[7]

FIGURE 20

And then we had another idea. I wanted to build the smallest guest bedroom you could make. How small of a room could you make that someone would still feel good in. So we decided to make one 7' x 7'. I hired Luckey again. I told him here's where it's going to go, and there's going to be a window on this wall. And I want to have a door. I want this room to change shape depending on how you are in it. What we came up with was a horizontal cylinder that revolves. He built it with several openings in it. The cylinder was 7' in diameter and revolved on wheels. It was made out of two skins of plywood and some hoops; he made the cylinder first and cut the holes out of it.

Sagan: So one way it's a bedroom, another way it's a sitting room?

Sellers: The bed was attached to the ceiling, the couch was attached over here, a chair over there, all the stuff that you need was [attached to] the inside surface of the cylinder. You'd walk in and you could dial it to what you wanted (FIGURE 21). When . . . the bed reached the bottom, the window [on the exterior wall of the house] suddenly lined up with the opening that you walked in on. And the two ends, which were stationary—one was a closet and one was a desk. So you could sit at the desk, and type and read, you could get up and move around and go to the closet. It became the most popular room in the house. Every guest needed to stay there, especially kids. They would get in it like it was a squirrel-cage and you'd hear this noise "bump-bump-bump-bump" and there would be four or five kids inside (laughs).

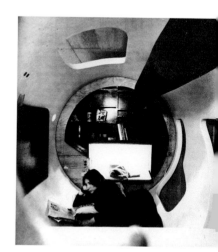

FIGURE 21

Sagan: You and Luckey figured out how to do this as you were going along.

Sellers: Yeah! You couldn't really figure it out without being in this little place. Once you were in there—it was the same as with the living room floor—once you were in there, it started to happen. The cues came out of the walls, the space, what was happening up there, what was happening down there, the texture of the materials

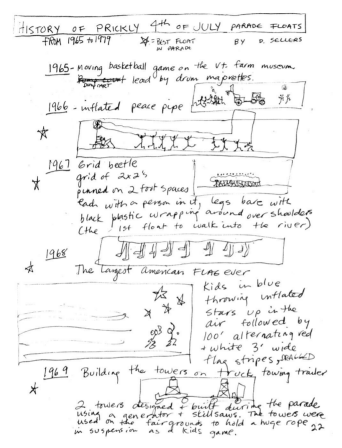

HISTORY OF PRICKLY 4th OF JULY PARADE FLOATS
FROM 1965 to 1979 ☆ = BEST FLOAT IN PARADE BY D. SELLERS

1965- Moving basketball game on the Vt. farm museum. lead by drum majorettes.

1966 - inflated peace pipe

☆ 1967 Grid beetle
grid of 2x2's
pinned on 2 foot spaces
each with a person in it, legs bare with
black plastic wrapping around over shoulders
(the 1st float to walk into the river)

1968
☆ The Largest American FLAG ever

Kids in blue
throwing inflated
stars up in the
air followed by
100' alternating red
+ white 3' wide
flag stripes, DRAGGED

1969 Building the towers on truck towing trailer
☆
2 towers designed + built during the parade
using a generator + skillsaws. The towers were
used on the fairgrounds to hold a huge rope
in suspension as a kids game. 22

FIGURE 22

and [other] materials you knew about. And there would be this discussion and it would go on and on and on, and all of a sudden, Boom! An idea would come out, and we'd make it. This way of dealing with stuff was best evidenced in our Fourth of July Parade floats.

Sagan: Tell me about that.

Sellers: Basically, you wait until the 3rd of July. Actually, the evening of the 2nd. You have a barbeque and you decide what it is you want to do. Everyone involved in making the float arrives and you decide what you want to do. It can be George Washington crossing the Delaware, or a rocket ship, or if there's been a flood, someone might suggest "How about a flood?" Then people would start rounding up materials and at 6:00 the next morning we would meet in the courtyard and make it. We would stay up all night the next night and then take it down to the parade. We started changing the Fourth of July parade here in Warren, from a dinky little parade (FIGURE 22).

Sagan: It is a big public event now.

Sellers: It's a huge public event. The parade was not very much back then; there were some horses and antique cars and it was not a big deal. So we decided to enter, because you could enter anything you wanted. While we were discussing what to do, the day before, we decided we definitely didn't want to watch the parade, we wanted to be in the parade because it would be more fun. And if we were going to be in it, we didn't want to be standing around. So we had a basketball game as our first float. We had the Hellenic Templettes versus some other team. We dressed up as Greek temples and the other team, I can't remember, was dressed up like Egyptians or something. We had two baskets on these carts with hoops and the whole thing moved. And the game would go on, so people could watch a basketball game (laughs). So that was something we knew you could make in one day; nobody knew what it was going to be the day before.

Sagan: Is that waiting as long as you can, or being creative as fast as you can?

Sellers: It's probably both. You know you've got to do it, and it's only going to last for two hours. If the float breaks the last step of the parade, that's good enough.

Now out of this developed a lot of theories on games and gamesmanship. One was the "Sever From Victory Theory," which was that you never want to win a game by a runaway score. You are not using your time properly. The ideal situation is to come from behind in the last 30 seconds and win by the least number of points possible. It means you are pushing your own limits all the way through. You can try the most risky things you can imagine, which have a higher chance of failing than anything else. So if you knew that you could make a basket, or score a touchdown, or push it into the net easily, you wouldn't bother doing that because it is too easy. You have to add some other feature to it. And as these things happen, you get closer and the other team is winning; you get within 30 seconds of the end, and you have managed to maintain being as close as possible. The satisfaction comes from one last amazing movement in the end. You have kind of been secretly holding your last cool move until the end and then surprising them with this spectacular trick.

Sagan: You put this in the context of the Fourth of July parade. Would you say this is also going on in the work that you have done in the design-build process?

Sellers: There is one aspect of it that does go on. The best part of the building isn't always available to be known before you are making it. So if you are working toward something, you always sense that final move hasn't been done yet. Otherwise it's boring. If everything you know is already known, there is no point in doing it.

You see, I had a classmate named Tom Kubota, and he gave me an unpublished thesis that he had found called *Intangible Content in Architecture.* It talks about irresolution in design. It is all about [Chinese philosopher] Lau Tzu, being there and not being there. That's why completing the square [is a useful symbol]. As soon as you complete a square when you draw a diagram, the square is dead. So what you do is you go all the way around and you don't really complete the square, you leave the observer to complete the square. That's when I began to see that irresolution in some ways has more beauty in it. Beauty or more inspirational quality than something that is completely done. Which is why I think there was such a reaction to Modernism. Because in Modernism, which came through Mies [van der Rohe] and some of the lesser architects who built all of these skyscrapers, they would complete the square. As it is completed it lost its personal energy. And that energy is an important thing to have. So I kept thinking, how do you get that energy and where does that energy come from, especially if a building is an extension of the human body. Then the human body has to have some interaction, and so in buildings I often would leave some parts of it totally unknown. To anybody. Much to the difficulty of some of my clients.

Sagan: Much to the difficulty?

Sellers: They had a hard time with that. Not all of them. Some of them loved it. Pinhead loved it. He loved the idea of discovering what it is you are making, while you are making it. And that as you are trying to create it, there are always these options and directions you can go off in, if you wanted too. And if you tried going off in a direction, you could come back with a residual of a failed direction. It could be left as a footprint in the building.

Endnotes

1. Douglas T. Hall and Fred I. Steele, "Self-Directed, Self-Relevant Learning," *The School Review* (The University of Chicago Press, November, 1971), Vol. 80, No. 1, 94–109

2. Chris Argyris, *Personality and Organization: The Conflict Between System and the Individual* (Harper, 1957)

3. Fritz Steele, *The Sense of Place* (Boston: CBI Publishing Co.,1981)

4. *Yale Alumni Magazine* (February, 1969), 28–35

5. "The Synthetic Environment," *Progressive Architecture* (October 1968), 180–201

6. "The Young Nomads," *Glamour* (November 1969), 175–177

7. "The Synthetic Environment," *Progressive Architecture,* 181 describes the ". . . contoured floor designed to form furniture that provides for changing activities of the occupants. Moss green carpeting, which is laid over two inches of urethane foam padding, upholsters the built-in plywood forms. The system replaces chairs, sofas, and tables, and also permits a flexibility in 'accommodating the body for conversational groupings,' as one observer points out. The walking texture is bouncy but does not affect one's general coordination. Recessed lighting has red gelatin lenses."

Tack House

Begun 1965
David Sellers with William Reineke, Ed Owre, and John Lucas
Warren, Vermont

PLATE 1: Tack House, 1966

Sibley/Pyramid House

Begun 1967
Started by William Reineke, completed by David Sellers
Warren, Vermont

PLATE 5: Sibley/Pyramid, 2008

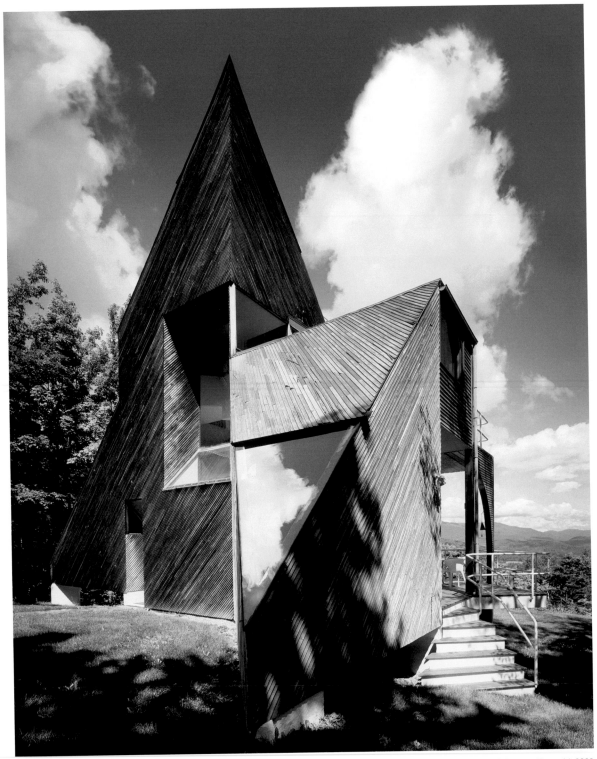

PLATE 6: Sibley/Pyramid, 2008

PLATES 7, 8: Sibley/Pyramid interiors, 2008

Bridge House

1966
David Sellers and Ed Owre
Warren, Vermont

PLATE 9: Bridge House
Construction, 1966

PLATE 10: Bridge House model, 1966

PLATE 11: Bridge House, 1967

PLATE 12: Bridge House, 1967

ARDEC House

ca. 1967
Peter Gluck
near Bolton Valley, Vermont

PLATE 13: ARDEC House, ca. 1967

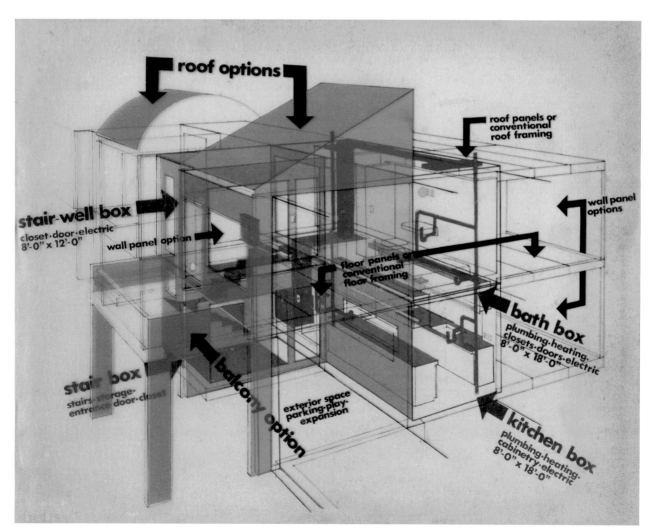

roof options

roof panels or conventional roof framing

stair-well box
closet·door·electric
8'-0" x 12'-0"

wall panel option

wall panel options

floor panels or conventional floor framing

bath box
plumbing·heating·
closets·doors·electric
8'-0" x 18'-0"

stair box
stairs·storage·
entrance door·closet

balcony option

exterior space
parking·play·
expansion

kitchen box
plumbing·heating·
cabinetry·electric
8'-0" x 18'-0"

PLATE 14: Peter Gluck, layered diagram, ARDEC House, ca. 1967

Lovejoy House

1970–71
Barry Simpson et al.
Lake Honnedaga, New York

PLATE 15: Lovejoy House, ca. 1971

PLATE 16: Lovejoy House, ca. 1971

Dimetrodon

Begun 1971
William Maclay, Jim Sanford, Richard Travers, et al.
Warren, Vermont

PLATE 17: Dimetrodon, 2008

PLATE 18: Dimetrodon, ca. 1971

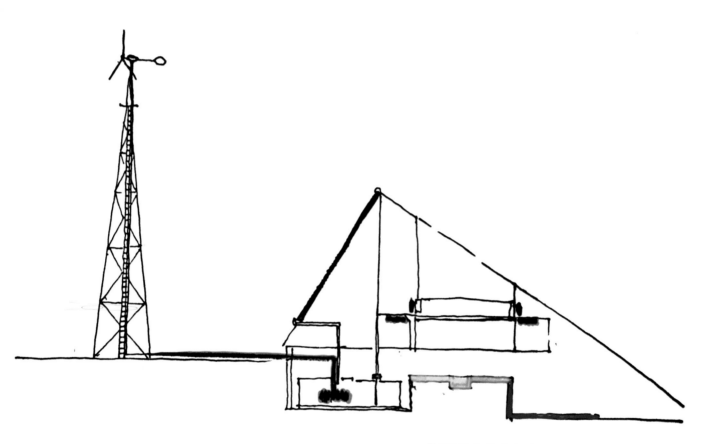

PLATE 19: Jim Sanford, schematic drawing of Dimetrodon, ca. 1971

PLATE 21: Dimetrodon, 2008

PLATE 20: (opposite) Dimetrodon, 2008

Anthos

1972
Charles Hosford, John Hausner, Tom Amsler, Charles Hagenah
Waitsfield, Vermont

PLATE 22: Anthos construction, 1972

PLATE 23: Anthos construction, 1972

PLATE 24: Anthos bathroom, 2008

PLATE 25: (opposite) Anthos interior, 2008

Goddard College Design Center, Sculpture and Painting Buildings

1971–1977
Goddard Construction Program students
with instructors David Sellers and John Mallery
Plainfield, Vermont

PLATE 26: Goddard College Design Center, 2008

PLATE 27: Goddard College Design Center interior, 2008

PLATE 28: Goddard College Design Center, top floor interior, 1971

PLATE 30: Goddard College
Arts Complex bridge, 2008

PLATE 29: Goddard College Sculpture Building interior, 2008

Warren Airport

Begun 1970
David Sellers and Charles Hosford,
built by Warren Ketchum
Warren, Vermont

PLATE 31: Warren Airport, 1970s

PLATE 33: Warren Airport, 1970s

PLATE 32: (opposite) Warren Airport, 1970s

PLATE 34: Warren Airport, 2008

Skidompha House

1973
David Sellers
Damariscotta, Maine

PLATE 35: Skidompha House construction, 1973

PLATE 36: Skidompha House construction, 1973

PLATE 37: Skidompha House, 1974

Seeking the Good Life: Vermont's Rural Resettlement in the Twentieth Century

Kevin Dann

In June 1931, two thousand people gathered at Centennial Field in Burlington to watch an evening performance of "Coming Vermont," Sarah Cleghorn's vision of farm, school, and church life in Vermont in the distant year 1981. The prophetic pageant was the finale of the Vermont Commission on Country Life's three-day conference to promote its manifesto, *Rural Vermont: A Program for the Future.* Along with fellow Vermont writers Dorothy Canfield Fisher, Zephine Humphrey, Bertha Oppenheim, and Walter Coates, Cleghorn was a member of the Commission's Committee on Traditions and Ideals, which was charged with charting a course for the state that would both protect Vermont traditional culture from the impending threats of automobile tourism, and use tourism as a means to nurture indigenous traditions. Their principal recommendation was to invite "authors, artists, college teachers, and others in the same general classification" to settle—or at least summer— in Vermont. In 1932 the Department of Publicity published Dorothy Canfield Fisher's *Vermont Summer Homes,* and over the next ten years mailed it out to tens of thousands of "desirable types" whom she was confident would "value what is worthwhile in our inheritance . . . help[ing] us hold to it." The pageant's final scene saw a local minister deliver a prayer, after which he raised the "banner of youth" and passed it to a young boy, advising him to carry it "onward and upward."[1]

A decade before the advent of the pageant's imagined 1981 future of a harmonious, Arcadian Vermont, *Playboy* magazine ran an article entitled "Taking Over Vermont," which envisioned a mere 225,000 "counterculturists" invading the state, figuring that this was the number needed to shift the politics and culture of the Green Mountain State from Yankee to Yippie.[2] Given the numbers mustered by the mobile counterculture for peace rallies and outdoor concerts, a considerable percentage of whom lived within an easy hitchhike to "the beckoning country," it seemed possible—possible enough to panic Yankees and transplanted Yippies alike. Indeed, Vermonters' fears of a hippie invasion had already led Governor Deane Davis to call a press conference to reassure Vermonters that "there is no visible cause for alarm at this point." Still, the Director of Public Safety and Health Colonel E. W. Corcoran asked the Vermont State Police to make surprise visits to communes, to help monitor the invasion. The Vermont League of Cities and Towns sponsored a conference to brief local officials on how to deal with the expected influx.[3]

But by 1971, the wave of hippie immigration had already begun to subside, after cresting in 1968 and 1969, when, in the wake of the assassinations of Martin Luther King and Robert Kennedy; urban race riots; and the police brutality at the 1968 Democratic National Convention, an enormous number of young people did migrate to Vermont, seeking refuge from both the ominous and uninhabitable city and the plastic, prefab suburbs, where—thanks to the relatively new technology of television—Betty Crocker and General Electric ruled as firmly as Mom and Dad. In the 1950s, hopeful Beats fleeing the suffocating postwar culture of containment had landed in urban areas—San Francisco, New York, Paris, or Tangiers. A decade later, the rise of environmental awareness made rural regions—especially northern California, the Southwest, and northern New England—the preferred destination for countercultural refugees. The recently completed southern section of I-91 helped point the banner of disaffected American youth towards Vermont.

The state was hardly a new destination for hopeful homesteaders: by 1932, when Vermont's most famous back-to-the-land proponents, Helen and Scott Nearing, had begun piling fieldstone to build their house in Jamaica, Vermont, New York City native Bertha Oppenheim was already orcharding in Basin Harbor; Zephine Humphrey (from Philadelphia) in Dorset; and Sam Ogden (from Elizabeth, N.J.) was taking up blacksmithing in Landgrove to supplement his farm income. Ogden published two books in the 1940s that presaged in some ways the Nearings' *Living the Good Life* (1954). *This Country Life*'s practical advice on building, beekeeping, cheesemaking, conservation, cooperatives, forestry, fruit, manure, mushrooms, and farm pests frequently was interrupted by philosophical flights-of-fancy that quoted cultural critics like George Santayana, Ortega y Gassett, Jacques Barzun, and Lewis Mumford. Ogden's bibliography listed Vermont Extension Service publications next to Ralph Borsodi's *This Ugly Civilization: A Study of the Quest for Comfort* (1929) and *The Flight from the City* (1933). When the Nearings would come to write *Living the Good Life,* Sam Ogden's books were in their bibliography.

Even a cursory glance at the biographies of the Nearings, Sam Ogden, or dozens of other celebrants of Vermont country life opens one up to the historical richness of the twentieth-century American back-to-the-land impulse, and to the realization that at its center is the perennial quest to solve the challenge of Vermont's state motto—"Freedom & Unity"—to create a home and community that honors individualism while embracing the social realm. *Living the Good Life*'s opening epigraphs—six quotes from authors ranging in time from 1616 to 1852—show the Nearings were fully conscious of just how old the tug-of-war was between city and country. Twentieth-century American life only intensified Petrarch's 14th-century invocation: "Arise, come, hasten, let us abandon the city." Scott Nearing had built his first cabin and grown his first organic garden in Arden, Delaware, in 1905. During their twenty years at Forest Farm in Jamaica, Vermont and then Harborside, Maine, the Nearings' aims and motivations encompassed the full spectrum of the rural resettlement impulse: an evangelical call to their fellow citizens to fully assess the nation's destructive and decaying social and ecological order; a peaceful, personal, political and economic alternative to the "plutocratic military oligarchy" that was increasingly gaining power; a program, through physical labor in nature, of intense self-cultivation. Their rejection of modern technology (the Nearings were famed for their scrupulous and muscular Luddism) and the authoritarian, militaristic state gave a decidedly antisocial cast to their experiment in living, which distinguished it from most other twentieth-century urban expatriates to Vermont.[4]

Though "individualist"—in the sense that it was comprised of childless couples or nuclear families—the pre-1960s wave of urban migrants to Vermont was, as the Commission on Country Life pageant and publication demonstrates, acutely community-oriented. When Sam Ogden came to Landgrove in 1929, he found a "miasma" over the town, and his homesteading efforts focused as much on community improvement as on self-cultivation. To make a living in the country—and to add and adapt one's talents to the neighborhood economy—Ogden studied, practiced, and then recommended to others a range of vocations: farming, woodworking, black-smithing, and doctoring. He was also perhaps the first of a long line of twentieth-century immigrants to cultivate and renew community by serving in the state legislature. Due to the depressed economic and social circumstances of his adopted community, Ogden's impulse was explicitly aimed at rural rehabilitation. More commonly, urban seekers of the good life in Vermont chose more prosperous communities, but wherever they settled, they worked assiduously to learn and then, as best as possible, imitate what they saw as the quaint, countrified ways of their neighbors.[5]

While their predecessor rural resettlers had emphasized "good government"—of self, home, farm, and community—the youthful communards of the 1960s more often rejected government, preferring Paul Goodman-style anarchism: decentralized, locally rooted communities linked together by affinity, and vitalized by modern but "miniaturized" technology. The 1960s brought a renewal of the early nineteenth-century communal endeavors, which were usually centered on contrarian politics, religion/spirituality, or alternative agriculture. The sheer number of Vermont communes (a 1970 census by the state estimated a range of 90–200; a 1971 national survey estimated 30,000 communes with a population of around 300,000) makes it difficult to generalize, but the experience of shared living spaces had been an important aspect of activists in both the civil rights and antiwar movements, and many brought this experience or aspiration with them when they came north to Vermont, discouraged by the apparent futility of their collective efforts at societal transformation in the cities.

Interesting alliances developed within both the national and Vermont back-to-the-land movements. Jungian therapist Jane Wheelwright bought a farm in Franklin, Vermont, not far from the Canadian border, and made it available with no restrictions on personal practices or land use. Four young couples with four children set out to live there as self-sufficiently as possible, eschewing fossil fuel dependency, and, whenever possible, substituting home-production and barter for purchasing goods. Like so many communes, the "Earthworks" commune aimed to heat and cook with wood; grow their own food; work with horses; and educate their own children. Between the deluge of guests (40 people arrived unannounced the first summer), inefficient labor organization (specialization was frowned upon as bourgeois, so *all* members were expected to learn how to perform all the necessary household tasks), and lack of essential rural skills, it was quickly apparent that they would produce at best half of their food, although they did manage to survive on very little cash.

Like previous urban ingénues, the communards experienced a steep learning curve: cows and horses and sheep got sick and the commune members who loved them were unable to care for them; potato bugs ravaged the potatoes, cabbage moth caterpillars the cabbage, hornworms the tomatoes; summer droughts dried up the well. At Earthworks, just as they were becoming much better organized, with abundant cordwood stacked in the shed, root crops and canned food laid by in the root cellar, and parasitic hangers-on ejected, a fire destroyed their house. Communards from other parts of the state—particularly Mullein Hill in Glover— came to help them rebuild; as with orthodox rural settlements, catastrophes often proved the most intense experience of true community.

The Wooden Shoe commune in Hartland, Vermont, founded by Dartmouth students in 1969, found its inspiration in political and social philosopher (and eventual transplant from New York City to Vermont) Murray Bookchin's *Anarchos* articles, which added an ecological apocalypticism to the traditional anarchist critique of the state. One of the commune's founders, Jake Guest, put it this way: "We've got to get back to small subsistence villages and tribes. Instead of huge sewage plants, we need thousands more outhouses and compost piles." When they first came to Hartland, they had neither outhouse nor compost pile; they were too busy hiring themselves out as housepainters and carpenters to build the decentralized, ecologically-sensitive infrastructure they envisioned. A year later, the Wooden Shoe (the name taken from the ultimate "small is beautiful" anarchist tool for remaking society—the *sabot,* a symbol associated with resistance to industrial drudgery) had moved back across the Connecticut River to an old farmhouse, restored with the help of a Yankee jack-of-all-trades, who—like so many Vermonters living up the road from the new wave of homesteaders—found himself adopted as a surrogate parent or grandparent.

Though at Wooden Shoe there still may have been a Ché Guevara poster on the living room wall, and Jefferson Airplane's "Volunteers" sounded from the stereo, the guiding sensibility was more in keeping with decentralist philosophers E.F. Schumacher and Wendell Berry. Members of the Red Clover commune— a media collective relocated to Putney from New York City—aimed to consolidate the state's countercultural communities of every stripe, as well as radicalize the natives, largely through publication of the magazine *Free Vermont.* They found varying degrees of support among the communards; the more successful communal experiments tended to put more energy into planting gardens than plotting revolution. Even Red Clover left its most lasting legacy in its own community rather than in state or national politics; Brattleboro's Liberation Garage (a free auto repair shop which operated for a brief time) and Common Ground restaurant (still operating) were founded by Red Clover members, and after moving north to Burlington to regroup as Green Mountain Red, members were pivotal in opening a free women's health clinic. The Maple Hill commune, in Plainfield, Vermont, found that simply adding competitively priced utilitarian items like mason jars and woodstoves became an effective avenue for building relationships with its neighbors.

Vermont had always been blessed by the fact that so many of the men and women who chose to go back to the land here were gifted writers; during the 1960s, Total Loss Farm in Guilford, Vermont emerged as *the* literary commune. Working as reporters for the Liberation News Service, founders Ray Mungo and Verandah Porche were in Washington, D.C. when Martin Luther King, Jr. was assassinated, and they were contacted by black militants asking for guns; machine-gun-wielding National Guardsmen had already filled the streets. When Porche and

Mungo decided to leave D.C., they opted to settle in Vermont. Scratching together a down payment on the $27,000 mortgage (Marty Jezer donated his Bar Mitzvah gift money), they were able to purchase the farmhouse of widow Rosie Franklin in Guilford's Packer Corner, near Brattleboro, Vermont. Mrs. Franklin's farm enabled Mungo, Porche, Jezer and the many friends who joined them over the years at Total Loss Farm to practice a wide variety of crafts and relationships with each other and the land.[6]

Despite its name, Total Loss Farm was one of the most successful communes in terms of longevity. The dozens of communes in Windham County and the 100+ around the state typically lasted only one or two winters, and usually a few members would regroup somewhere else—California, New Mexico, or in another Vermont location. After six months of communal living at Sunrise Hill in Conway, Massachusetts, some members moved to Bryn Athyn, near South Strafford, Vermont. From August 1967 to December 1969, a crazy quilt collection of people came and went, under the patronage of Woody Ransom, who had originally bought the farm as an artist's retreat for himself and his wife. The promise of the farm's name (Welsh for "hill of unity") was never realized; after Ransom's marriage broke up, it became the summer retreat and training ground—for karate and target shooting—of the "Motherfuckers," the self-appointed bodyguards of East Village hipsterdom. In December 1969, after one Bryn Athyn member died of hepatitis and three others contracted the disease, the commune broke up, then resurrected as "Rockbottom" a mile away, in a fully applianced house with Ransom—who had renounced anarchism for the behaviorally-engineered autocracy of B.F. Skinner's *Walden Two*—as benevolent dictator.

Almost without exception, communes received as much hospitality as they practiced themselves toward their host communities. Ruth Clark, a dairy farming neighbor of the Johnson's Pasture and Total Loss Farm communes, recalls that:

> All the people I knew didn't mind them at all. The ones we knew were friendly. They had a lot of good ideas—they were clever kids. They wanted to get back to the land and didn't have enough expertise or money to make much of it. . . It was what was going on in other places, it was just like these were 'our hippies.' Other places had 'their' hippies, and these were 'our' hippies.[7]

But more often than not, commune members violated a host of community norms—the same ones that held in their hometowns, and which they were consciously seeking to escape. One Guilford resident put it quite plainly:

> There are a lot of rules in a rural community, sort of unspoken, unwritten rules. You don't go into town to do your grocery shopping in your farm clothes; you changed into clean clothes. . . if you slouch into town with manure on your boots, that's kind of low class to the country people. But with the ones who lived on the communes there was a real rebellion against middle class values, and that included perhaps even being clean.[8]

Long hair was perhaps the most ubiquitous banner of youthful rebellion in the 1960s. In 1970, Brattleboro High School banned its male athletes from sporting long hair, igniting a fiery local culture war. Among Guilford residents, there is considerable folklore about the subject of hair; one popular story says that stocks were placed in front of the Town Hall, and when local people caught a long-haired hippie, they would put them in the stocks and shave their hair. Another version (from Putney) has it that a few local men drove around town with bathtubs in the bed of their pickup trucks, and would grab hippies, cut their hair, and then throw them in the bathtub.[9]

Though many of the '60s-era communards came to Vermont for the freedom to raise their children in an environment more conducive to their particular values, they were all too often insensitive to what their presence meant for their neighbors' children. A member of the Total Loss commune recalled that when she had first moved in, a neighboring farmer confessed to her his concern that his son "would come see what we were about." Most Vermonters did not wish to see their sons and daughters exposed to the excesses that the mass media was so fond of publicizing to the nation.[10]

The 60s communes explosively expressed the perennial tension between anarchy and autocracy. The most beautiful, pleasing cultural productions of that era are all marked by some measure of balance between the irresistible freedom of formlessness and the necessary rigor of form. It is on every page of the *Whole Earth Catalog,* which threw its exuberant intellectual net around Whole Systems, Land Use, Shelter, Industry, Craft, Community, Nomadics, Communications, and Learning, and, in the fully democratic, craft-apprenticing spirit of the times, concluded with brief instructions on how to make your own *Whole Earth Catalog.*

A hint of chaos ran through the elegantly designed antinomianism
of the *Catalog*'s last gasp, the *Whole Earth Epilog,* in the form of the madcap
adventures of "Divine Right's Trip," which ran like a cartoon flip-book down in the
lower right-hand corner of its 447 pages, before expending itself in one final grok on
the back cover, the text swimming around an ouroboros—a pair of dragons swallowing
each others' tails. The opening pair of pages of the *Epilog*—at its 15th printing in
the fall of 1974, it had already sold over 1.5 million copies—are devoted to the ideas
of R. Buckminster Fuller. There is a photograph of "Bucky" on Hippie Hill in San
Francisco in 1968, surrounded by admiring longhairs; below are drawings of his
Dymaxion car, and some stanzas from his epic poem, "No More Secondhand God":

> I see God in
> The instruments and the mechanisms that
> work
> reliably. . .

Reliably working systems of living is what the communards dreamed
of creating, but usually their reach exceeded their grasp. The communes tended to
produce ephemeral, improvised housing—tarpaulined teepees, dilapidated barns,
and recycled school buses that lasted a summer at best. Draft horses gave suburban
expatriates a thrill at first, but when whiffletrees and leather harnesses snapped, the
novice agrarians were often left running to neighboring farmers for advice on repairs.
The tragedies of the communal era—deaths from woodstove-ignited housefires,
chainsaw injuries, construction accidents—were more often than not due to exuberant,
anarchic youths seeking the good life through human-scale technology failing to
effectively master that technology.

For Dave Sellers, Bill Reinecke, and the couple of dozen architecture
students who in 1966 took up their invitation to come get practical building
experience in the Mad River Valley, the decentralized, libertarian physical and
social landscape of Vermont offered a place to make healthy, helpful mistakes while
learning. In scattered forest openings, away from the architectural constraints of
village propriety, they built futuristic homes without violating the villagescape. The
surrounding mountains called forth soaring structures whose rooflines, entranceways,
windows, and decks, for all their unconventionality, seemed to fit the place.

Though founded principally as an entrepreneurial initiative, Prickly
Mountain (named for one green architectural student's backside encounter with a

patch of bramble) shared with Vermont's intentional communities a commitment to sustainable living and social ecology. A 75-acre commons was set aside, and the Potato Road Association formed to steward the neighborhood away from the temptation for quick profit, toward community-minded consideration of the future. When Penn architecture students Bill Maclay, Jim Sanford, and Dick Travers arrived at Prickly in 1970, they renewed and quickened the founding impulses of residential design that used renewable energy and promoted community. Their "Dimetrodon," though named for a dinosaur, was anything but, its flexibility allowing it to survive and thrive through a tumultuous time that saw most of its cohort go down to extinction.

Vermont's lack of building codes and its relatively laissez-faire *civitas*—particularly the paucity of police—gave space for both communal and individual countercultural experiments to flourish or fail on their own merits. Like the pioneers who had proceeded them—not just Sam Ogden, the Nearings, and the Prickly Mountain architects, but every wave of ex-urban immigration to Vermont since the end of the American Revolution—the '60s homesteaders performed a delicate alchemical dance between serendipity and design; frontier lawlessness and village authority; Freedom and Unity. "We thought we wanted a commune, but what we were really looking for was *community,*" declared one veteran communard.

Driving down Route 100 or while out walking a dirt road, you may come upon some wild, wonderful architectural structures, or a suite of raised beds, laid out in a mandala pattern, but now overgrown with thistle and bramble and young popple. These—like dozens of Vermont inventions and institutions, from Vermont Castings stoves and Gardener's Supply catalogs, to Bread & Puppet Theater, Goddard College, Yestermorrow Design/Build School, the Vermont Studio Center, the National Organic Farming Association, and even Ben & Jerry's!—are all rich legacies of the latest impulse to seek the good life in a good and gracious place.

Endnotes

1. *Burlington Free Press,* June 18, 1931, p. 6; Henry F. Perkins, et al., *Rural Vermont: A Program for the Future* (Burlington, Vermont: Vermont Commission on Country Life, 1931)

2. Richard Pollak, "Taking Over Vermont," *Playboy,* April 1972

3. *Burlington Free Press*, May 19, 1971

4. Scott and Helen Nearing, *Living the Good Life* (Harborside, Maine, 1954), viii

5. The Vermont "Country Life" literature is extensive, ranging from romantic—Bertha Oppenheim's *Winged Seeds* (1923) and Frederick Van de Water's 1940 *The Circling Year*—to comic—Elswyth Thane's *Reluctant Farmer* (1950) and Edmund Fuller's *Successful Calamity: A Writer's Follies on a Vermont Farm* (1966)— to utilitarian—Sam Ogden's *How to Grow Food for Your Family* (1942)

6. In both the memoirs by members and the extensive media coverage of Total Loss Farm and nearby Johnson's Pasture communes, no mention is ever made of the fact that since at least the 1930s, the towns where they were sited—Guilford and Putney—had been home to expatriated artists and communitarians. The Experiment in International Living (founded in 1932), Putney School (1935), Windham College (1951), and Antioch University New England (1964) were founded by this earlier wave of immigrants to the area. A century and a half before these 20th-century impulses, the same area had been host to one of Vermont's— and America's—most radical communitarians, John Humphrey Noyes.

7. Interviews conducted by Reid R. Frazier, from his excellent 2002 University of Vermont M.A. thesis, *1960s Communes in Southern Vermont;* 167, 177–178

8. Ibid.

9. Frazier, *1960s Communes in Southern Vermont,* 174–175

10. Ibid., 168. The teen whose father expressed his concern about the Total Loss communes' unconventional lifestyles became friendly with commune members, and went on to become the first openly gay state legislator in Vermont. (Ibid., 169)

Covers, Inside Front Cover:

Jim Westphalen

Inside Back Cover:

Potato Bugle Newsletter, Vol. 1, No. 1, p. 22.
Courtesy of David Sellers

Color Plates

1   Progressive Architecture, "Architecture
    Swings Like a Pendulum Do," May 1966,
    p. 152. Reprinted with permission of *Architect*
    and Hanley Wood LLC

2   Courtesy of Candy Barr

3–8   Jim Westphalen

9   *Progressive Architecture,* "Architecture
    Swings Like a Pendulum Do," May 1966,
    p. 151. Reprinted with permission of *Architect*
    and Hanley Wood LLC

10   Life Magazine, "Ski-House Tree House,"
    March 24, 1967, pp. 84–85

11   *Progressive Architecture,* "Architecture
    Swings Like a Pendulum Do," May 1966,
    p. 157. Reprinted with permission of *Architect*
    and Hanley Wood LLC

12   *Life* Magazine, "Ski-House Tree House,"
    March 24, 1967, p. 86

13–14   © Peter L. Gluck and Partners, Architects

15–16   Barry Simpson, courtesy of Barry Simpson

17   Jim Westphalen

18–19   Courtesy of Jim Sanford

20–21   Jim Westphalen

22–23   John Hausner, courtesy of John Hausner

24–27   Jim Westphalen

28   *Progressive Architecture,* "Organic Architecture
    at Goddard College," November 1971, p. 3.
    Reprinted with permission of *Architect* and
    Hanley Wood LLC

29–30   Jim Westphalen

31–33   Courtesy of David Sellers

34   Jim Westphalen

35–37   David Sellers, courtesy of David Sellers

Sagan Essay Figures

1   Jim Westphalen

2   Chris Dissinger

3   Courtesy of David Sellers

4   Danny Sagan

5   *Progressive Architecture,* "Architecture
    Swings Like a Pendulum Do," May 1966,
    p. 157. Reprinted with permission of *Architect*
    and Hanley Wood LLC

6   Danny Sagan

7   *Valley Reporter,* January 1978. Courtesy of
    David Sellers

8   *Life* Magazine, "Ski-House Tree House,"
    March 24, 1967, p. 86

9   *Progressive Architecture,* "Architecture
    Swings Like a Pendulum Do," May 1966,
    p. 157. Reprinted with permission of *Architect*
    and Hanley Wood LLC

10–11   © Peter L. Gluck and Partners, Architects

12   *Progressive Architecture,* "Architecture
    Swings Like a Pendulum Do," May 1966,
    p. 153. Reprinted with permission of *Architect*
    and Hanley Wood LLC

13–15   Barry Simpson, courtesy of Barry Simpson

16   Courtesy of Jim Sanford

17   *Progressive Architecture,* "Organic Architecture
    at Goddard College," November 1971, p. 6.
    Reprinted with permission of *Architect* and
    Hanley Wood LLC

18   Vance Smith, courtesy of Vance Smith

19   Photographer: Gary Hall; courtesy of
    John Connell

Sellers Interview Figures

1–2   *Progressive Architecture,* "Systems/Kits,"
    October 1968, p. 180. Reprinted with
    permission of *Architect* and Hanley Wood LLC

3   Potato Bugle Newsletter, Vol. 1, No. 1, p. 22.
    Courtesy of David Sellers